D1709241

EMMA S. CLARK MEMORIAL LIBRARY
SETAUKET, L.I., NEW YORK 11733

The Pennsylvania Colony

Bob Italia

ABDO Publishing Company

visit us at
www.abdopub.com

Published by ABDO Publishing Company, 4940 Viking Drive, Edina, Minnesota 55435.
Copyright © 2001 by Abdo Consulting Group, Inc. International copyrights reserved in all
countries. No part of this book may be reproduced in any form without written permission from
the publisher.

Printed in the United States.

Cover Photo Credit: North Wind Picture Archives
Interior Photo Credits: North Wind Picture Archives (pages 11, 13, 15, 17, 19, 21, 25, 27, 29);
    Corbis (pages 7, 9, 23)

Contributing Editors: Tamara L. Britton, Kate A. Furlong, and Christine Fournier
Book Design and Graphics: Neil Klinepier

Library of Congress Cataloging-in-Publication Data

Italia, Bob, 1955-
    The Pennsylvania Colony / Bob Italia.
        p. cm. -- (The colonies)
    Includes index.
    ISBN 1-57765-588-5   2427440
        1. Pennsylvania--History--Colonial period, ca. 1600-1775--Juvenile literature. [1.
Pennsylvania--History--Colonial period, ca. 1600-1775.] I. Title. II. Series.

F152 .I83 2001
974.8'02--dc21

                                                                2001022785

Contents

Penn's Land of Woods

Before European colonists arrived, Native Americans lived in Pennsylvania. Dutch and Swedish colonists were Pennsylvania's first European settlers. Then the English seized the land. England's king gave the land to William Penn.

Penn wanted Pennsylvania's colonists to have many freedoms and rights. So he wrote Pennsylvania's first **constitution**. Men participated in the government.

At first, relations between the Native Americans and colonists were good. But then they fought over land. Eventually, the Native Americans were forced out of Pennsylvania.

Pennsylvania played an important role in the **American Revolution**. The **Continental Congresses** met in Philadelphia.

After the war, Pennsylvania became the second state. Today, Pennsylvania is a leading manufacturing and industrial center of the United States.

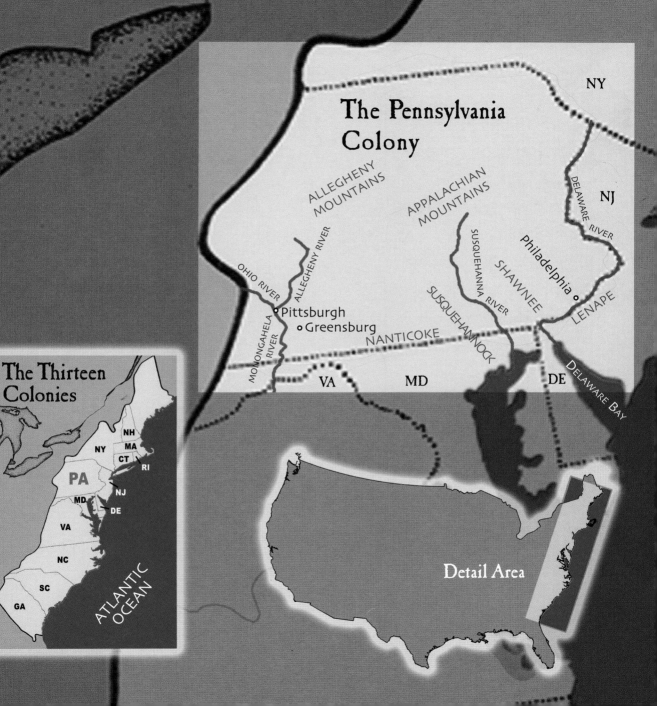

The Pennsylvania Colony

NY

ALLEGHENY MOUNTAINS

APPALACHIAN MOUNTAINS

DELAWARE RIVER

NJ

OHIO RIVER

ALLEGHENY RIVER

SUSQUEHANNA RIVER

SHAWNEE

Philadelphia

MONONGAHELA RIVER

Pittsburgh

Greensburg

SUSQUEHANNOCK

NANTICOKE

LENAPE

VA

MD

DE

Delaware Bay

The Thirteen Colonies

NH
NY
MA
CT
RI
PA
NJ
MD
DE
VA
NC
SC
GA

ATLANTIC OCEAN

Detail Area

Early History

Pennsylvania is a state on the mid-Atlantic coast. The western part of the state is mountainous. The eastern part is a plateau that slopes down to the Delaware River.

Native Americans lived in Pennsylvania thousands of years before the European colonists arrived. These tribes included the Lenape (luh-NA-pay), Nanticoke (NAN-tih-kohk), Shawnee, and Susquehannock (sus-kwuh-HAN-uk).

The Lenape, Nanticoke, and Shawnee were **Algonquian** (al-GON-kwee-an) speaking tribes. The Susquehannock spoke Iroquoian (ear-oh-KWOY-an).

In each tribe, the men hunted and fished. The women farmed. They grew corn, squash, beans, and tobacco.

The Native Americans lived in houses made from sapling frames. They covered the frames with mats made of reeds or bark. They made tools and weapons from stone, wood, and bark. Native Americans created dugout canoes from large tree trunks. They also made clothing from animal skins.

Native Americans make a dugout canoe.

First Explorers

Giovanni da Verrazzano (gee-oh-VAH-nee dah ver-rah-ZAH-noh) sailed up the coast of North America in 1524. In 1608, Captain John Smith traveled from the Virginia Colony up the Susquehanna River.

In 1609, Henry Hudson sailed into Delaware Bay. He was looking for trade routes for the Dutch government. Hudson's reports led the Dutch to send other explorers.

In 1614, Dutchman Cornelius May explored the region. In 1615, Cornelius Hendricksen sailed up the Delaware River to what is now Philadelphia.

The Dutch explorers established trading posts in the area. They traded with the Native Americans. The Native Americans traded animal furs for cloth, weapons, cooking pots, and other goods.

Native Americans trade furs with the colonists.

Settlement

Colonists from Sweden created Pennsylvania's first permanent settlement. They settled near present-day Wilmington, Delaware. They called their settlement New Sweden. In 1643, the governor of New Sweden established a capital at Tinicum Island near present-day Philadelphia.

The Dutch did not like the Swedish settlement. They thought it interfered with their trading posts. So in 1655, the Dutch governor seized New Sweden.

England's king, Charles II, did not like the Dutch colony. It was between his Virginia and New England colonies. So in 1664, English soldiers seized the Dutch colonies. In 1681, King Charles gave the land to William Penn.

Penn was a **Quaker**. He wanted a place where Quakers could worship freely. He also wanted people to have personal and property rights and self-government.

Penn called his land Sylvania, which means *woods*. King Charles added Penn to the name to honor Sir William Penn, Penn's father. He was a respected admiral in the English Navy.

In October 1682, Penn arrived in Pennsylvania on the ship *Welcome*. He created Pennsylvania's three original counties. By the time he returned to England in 1684, the colony was well established.

William Penn arrives in Pennsylvania.

11

Government

Penn wrote Pennsylvania's first **constitution**. He called it the Frame of Government. It guaranteed freedom of worship, protection of property, and trial by jury. It created a council and assembly elected by the people.

The council had 72 members. It created laws and courts, founded cities, and established schools. The assembly had 200 members. It approved or rejected laws created by the council. England's king also had to approve the laws. The first assembly met on December 4, 1682.

The second assembly met in 1683. It revised the Frame of Government. It created a council with 18 members and an assembly with 36. It also shortened the time between the proposal of a bill and the meeting of the assembly to approve it.

In 1692, England's King William III and Queen Mary II took away Penn's right to govern the colony. They thought he was a disloyal citizen. But Penn

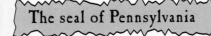

The seal of Pennsylvania

convinced them he was loyal. They made him governor again in 1694.

Pennsylvania's government changed again in 1696. Colonists adopted a new **constitution** called Markham's Frame. It gave the assembly power to make laws.

In 1701, Penn prepared the Charter of Privileges. Under the charter, only the assembly could make laws. The assembly became independent of the governor. And it scheduled its own sessions. The charter remained in force until 1776.

The Frame of Government

The FRAME of the
GOVERNMENT
OF THE
Province of Pennſilvania
IN
AMERICA
Together with certain
LAWS
Agreed upon in England
BY THE
GOVERNOUR
AND
Divers FREE-MEN of the aforeſaid
PROVINCE.

To be further Explained and Confirmed there by the firſt
Provincial Council and General Aſſembly that ſhall
be held, if they ſee meet.

Printed in the Year MDCLXXXII.

REDUCED FAC-SIMILE OF TITLE OF "THE FRAME
OF GOVERNMENT."

Life in the Colony

Pennsylvania's early colonists had to survive on their own. Men worked in the fields or forests. They raised livestock. Boys helped their fathers with chores.

Women spent their time caring for their family. They cooked meals and made clothing. Girls helped their mothers by doing household chores.

But the colonists did not work all the time. Religious holidays were important to them. But **Quakers** did not approve of dancing or going to plays. They believed it was a sin to waste anything, even time.

English Quakers were the largest group to settle in the Pennsylvania Colony. Other English settlers were Anglican. Both groups settled in the southeastern counties. These counties became thriving agricultural and commercial areas.

Thousands of Germans also came to the Pennsylvania Colony. They settled in the interior counties. They were called **Pennsylvania Dutch**. They became successful farmers.

Quakers leave their meetinghouse after attending services.

Making a Living

The Pennsylvania Colony had many natural resources. Colonists grew much food in the rich farmland. Wheat and corn were the main crops.

Often, the colonists had enough food to sell to other colonies and countries. But the colonists usually did not have much money. They **bartered** for the goods and services they needed.

The colony's many rivers also contributed to the **economy**. The colonists built sawmills and gristmills on the waterways. The sawmills sawed trees into lumber. The gristmills ground wheat and corn into flour.

Pennsylvania's land provided iron ore. Blacksmiths worked iron into finished products, such as horseshoes, pots, and nails. The blacksmith became an important member of the community.

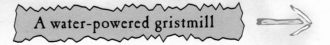
A water-powered gristmill

Leather tanning also became an important industry. It was hard to find a town in the Pennsylvania Colony that did not have a tanyard near it.

Food

Early Pennsylvania colonists grew corn, oats, rye, barley, peas, squash, turnips, potatoes, and wheat. Some grew onions and tobacco. They also raised sheep, cows, and pigs. Apple orchards provided fruit for eating, and cider for drinking.

Farmers also grew vegetables in kitchen gardens. They grew herbs and spices to flavor their foods. The colonists also used herbs to prevent sickness.

Colonists added to their meals with food from the forests. They hunted rabbits, deer, partridges, wild turkeys, and bears. They caught fish in the many rivers and waterways.

The colonists had to preserve food for the long winter months. They salted and pickled meats for storage. Apples buried in the dry dirt of the fruit cellar lasted for months. A **springhouse** provided the necessary coldness to keep milk fresh for more than a day. It also kept butter from melting.

The wild turkey

Clothing

Colonists grew flax on their farms. They also raised sheep for wool. The women made the flax fibers and wool shearings into clothing.

First they spun the wool shearings or flax fibers into thread on a spinning wheel. Some of the thread was knitted into socks, hats, scarves, and mittens.

Then, the women wove some of the thread into cloth on a loom. They used the cloth to make clothing and other household linens. They sewed everything by hand.

The women used leather to make everyday items such as trousers, aprons, and buckets. Leather was stronger than cloth and lasted longer. And it was readily available from the leather tanneries.

Many **Quakers** believed fancy clothing distracted people from their spiritual life. So they wore simple clothing. Men wore heavy **breeches** and linen shirts. Women wore plain dresses.

Wealthy colonists bought fancy clothing imported from England.

Homes

Pennsylvania's first colonists built their own homes. Fathers and sons did the work. In later periods, all the men of the community built houses for newcomers.

First, the men dug the cellar. Then they built a stone foundation over the cellar hole. The men laid square-**hewn** logs directly on top of the stone foundation. They usually constructed the floor of puncheons, which were logs with one side hewn flat.

Iron nails were expensive and hard to find. So colonists did not use them often. Instead, they used wooden pegs.

Colonists covered outside walls with clapboards. Some colonists whitewashed the clapboards. Other colonists covered outside walls with brick or stucco. They also covered the inside walls with plaster or whitewash.

The cracks between the logs were called chinks. Colonists filled the chinks with a mixture of clay and straw. This kept cold air and animals out.

If a house had windows, they were often small. Glass was expensive. So colonists covered windows with oilpaper or cloth.

The first homes had only one room. Sometimes, colonists had a **loft** for storage or for the children to sleep in. To get to the loft, children climbed pegs pounded into the wall or used a ladder.

This early log cabin has chinks that have been filled with clay.

Children

Most families had many children. The children helped work in the house and on the farm. Boys did farm chores. They cleared and plowed fields, planted and harvested crops, and cared for farm animals.

Girls cooked, preserved food, cared for younger children, cleaned the house, washed the clothes, and tended the garden. They also milked cows, churned butter, and made cheese.

Children helped their mothers make soap every spring. They made it in a large kettle over an outdoor fire.

Quakers did not believe in extensive education. But they knew that basic education was important to society. So the Frame of Government called for the creation of public schools.

Colonial children help their mother make soap by gathering wood for the fire.

Native Americans

The Native Americans and the early Pennsylvania colonists got along well. Penn saw the Native Americans as fellow human beings. He did not want to harm them.

Penn made a treaty of friendship with the Native Americans shortly after he arrived in the colony. He paid them for the land King Charles had given him.

The Native Americans trusted Penn. They were friendly and generous to the colonists. But later, the colonists mistreated the Native Americans. They cheated them out of land. And many were killed in battles and wars.

In 1754, the French and Indian War began. The French and English fought for control of land in America. Many Native Americans fought on the French side.

In 1763, Ottawa chief Pontiac led many Native Americans in the Battle of Bushy Run. They fought against the English near present-day Greensburg. The English won the battle. That same year, England won the war.

Pennsylvania colonists bought land from the Native Americans in the Fort Stanwix Treaty of 1768. This treaty settled most of the colony's land **disputes** with the Native Americans. The Native Americans eventually moved westward, gradually leaving Pennsylvania.

William Penn signs a treaty with the Native Americans.

The Road to Statehood

By the 1770s, the Pennsylvania Colony was the third largest English colony in North America. Philadelphia was the largest English-speaking city in the world outside London.

But by then, England had imposed new taxes and trade laws on its American colonies. The colonies united to oppose these actions.

The First **Continental Congress** met in Philadelphia on September 5, 1774. It voted to stop all trade with England.

The **American Revolution** began in April 1775. That May, the Second Continental Congress met in Philadelphia. The delegates voted for independence from England.

On July 4, 1776, Congress adopted the Declaration of Independence in the Pennsylvania State House in Philadelphia. It said the colonies were independent states. Pennsylvania's first state convention was held in the State House at the same time.

In 1783, the colonies won the war. Pennsylvania became the second state on December 12, 1787.

Today, Pennsylvania is a leading manufacturing and industrial center of the United States. It makes chemicals, processed foods, and electrical equipment. It is also one of the nation's most historic states.

The Founding Fathers sign the Declaration of Independence in the Pennsylvania State House. The Pennsylvania State House is now called Independence Hall.

TIMELINE

1524 - Giovanni da Verrazzano sails up North America's coast
1608 - John Smith travels up Susquehanna River
1609 - Henry Hudson sails into Delaware Bay
1614 - Cornelius May explores the Pennsylvania area
1615 - Cornelius Hendricksen sails up the Delaware River to Philadelphia
1643 - Swedish explorers establish New Sweden
1655 - Dutch seize New Sweden
1664 - English seize Dutch land
1681 - King Charles II gives land to William Penn
1682 - Penn arrives in Pennsylvania Colony; first assembly meets under Frame of Government
1683 - Second assembly meets, revises Frame of Government
1692 - William and Mary strip Penn of right to govern Pennsylvania Colony
1694 - Penn regains governorship
1696 - Markham's Frame of government enacted
1701 - Charter of Privileges government enacted
1754 - French and Indian War begins, ends nine years later
1763 - Battle of Bushy Run
1768 - Fort Stanwix Treaty signed
1774 - First Continental Congress meets
1775 - American Revolution begins
1776 - Declaration of Independence signed
1783 - American Revolution ends
1787 - Pennsylvania becomes second state

Glossary

Algonquian - a family of Native American languages spoken from Labrador, Canada, to the Carolinas, and westward to the Great Plains.

American Revolution - 1775-1783. A war between England and its colonies in America. The colonists won their independence and created the United States.

barter - to trade goods and services for other goods and services without using money.

breeches - tight-fitting, short pants.

Constitution - the laws that govern the United States. Each state has a constitution, too.

Continental Congress - the body of representatives who spoke and acted on behalf of the thirteen colonies.

dispute - an argument or disagreement.

economy - the way a colony uses its money, goods, and natural resources.

hew - to shape with a heavy cutting instrument, such as an ax.

loft - the upper story of a house or building, often used for storage.

Pennsylvania Dutch - people of German ancestry who immigrated to Pennsylvania. The name comes form the word *Deutsch*, which means "German" in the German language.

Quaker - a member of the religious group called the Society of Friends.

springhouse - a small building built over a spring and used for storing meat or dairy products.

Web Sites

Spotlight on Pennsylvania History
http://www.phmc.state.pa.us/spotlight/spotlight.htm
Learn more about William Penn and Pennsylvania's historic past at the official Pennsylvania state site.

Colonial Pennsylvania Plantation
http://www.delcohistory.org/colonialplantation/
See an early Pennsylvania farmhouse, learn about farmwork and family roles, see how food is preserved in a springhouse, and more!

These sites are subject to change. Go to your favorite search engine and type in Pennsylvania Colony for more sites.

31

Index